Servants
of the land

Servants
of the land

৪৯

God, Family, and Farm

THE TRINITY OF
BELGIAN ECONOMIC FOLKWAYS
IN SOUTHWESTERN MINNESOTA

Joseph A. Amato

CROSSINGS
PRESS

Longmont, Colorado   *Marshall, Minnesota*

Servants of the Land is a Crossings Press publication

Illustration by Polly Christensen.
Maps and photographs reproduced by permission of Southwest Minnesota Historical Center, Southwest State University, Marshall, MN 56258

First edition © 1990
Second revised edition © 1991 by Crossings Press

Published and distributed in the United States of America by:

Crossings Press   Crossings Press
P.O. Box 764   1646 Bowen Street
Marshall, MN 56258   Longmont, CO 80501

Library of Congress CIP data is available upon request from the Library of Congress.

ISBN 0-9614119-2-9

Printed and bound in the United States of America

The paper used in this publication meets the requirements of the American National Standard for Permanence of Paper for Printed Library Materials Z39.48-1984.

10   9   8   7   6   5   4   3   2

Contents

Acknowledgments

This work could not have been written without the help of Janice Louwagie, Coordinator of the Southwest Minnesota Historical Center. Critical readings by several members of the Louwagie family were important as were the constructive and encouraging remarks by John Radzilowski and Professor Eugen Weber. Patty Schmidt did much to improve the manuscript and Jeanne Barker, Lyon County Recorder, and her staff taught me some of the mysteries of title searches.

The very most special thanks go to Scott and Mira Perrizo, who have supported my writings over a decade, bringing to them not only their enthusiasm but their knowledge of books and book production. To this work Scott not only brought his talent, as he did in the design and production of my *Death Book, Ethics, Living or Dead?*, and *Guilt and Gratitude,* but he welcomed *Servants of the Land* as the first publication of our new press, Crossings Press, which will be dedicated to themes of human and cultural migration and the people and world of southwestern Minnesota. Also gratitude is owed to many others for the publication of *Servants of the Land.* It is owed to Thaddeus Radzilowski, his son, John Radzilowski, and Kevin Stroup, who were instrumental in founding the Society for the Study of Local and Regional History, which has chosen to make *Servants of the Land* its first official publication and a significant part of its first annual conference. In turn, thanks are owed to the president of Southwest State University, Douglas Treadway, the Southwest State History Department and its chair, David Nass, and the university's History Club, Pi Gamma Mu, and the Southwest Educational Cooperative Service Unit whose generosity and cooperation continue to be a valued asset for our university and region. The Minnesota Humanities Commission, represented by Mark Gleason, played a unique and valuable role by encouraging and funding the first annual conference of the Society for the Study of Regional and Local History.

J.A.A.

Getting and Keeping the Land

A part of the lore of agricultural regions throughout the world concerns those groups of farmers who succeed on the land, and those who fail.

It is no different in Lyon County, located in the southwestern corner of Minnesota. Lyon County sits on what was once the northwestern corner of the tall grass prairie, approximately sixty miles from both the South Dakota and Iowa borders. Here the horizon is great, spaces are vast, and seasons are extreme; temperatures can range from $-30°$ Fahrenheit on the coldest days of winter to over $100°$ on the most blistering days of summer. Only river valleys and groves of trees located on the north and northwest perimeters of farm sites protect one from winter's sharpest winds. Here the soil is black and rich. It is still approximately 12 inches deep even after a century of modern agriculture, with its compacting machinery and the inevitable wind erosion that accompanies modern agriculture's practice. The topsoil was estimated to have been twenty-four to thirty inches deep when the settlers came and began to plow the land and drain the marshes, sloughs, and the small lakes that covered this area and supported an incredibly rich eco-system. Beginning in parts of the western tier of townships in Lyon County and continuing on into the Dakotas, the elevation of the land is higher, the climate drier, the soils sandier, and the land much poorer for farming.

Lyon County, like much of the trans-Mississippi west, was opened in the post-Civil War period by the government and the railroads to feed the growing populations of the nation's new urban centers. After the army suppressed the great Dakota Sioux uprising of 1862, which killed over five hundred white settlers in southwestern Minnesota, the Dakota were removed from Minnesota, opening the door to the complete settlement of the region. By 1890, railroad lines crisscrossed southwestern Minnesota. Railroad villages and towns uniformly divided up the countryside. In less than two decades Lyon County, like so much of the rest of the Midwest, was put in the service of feeding expanding American and European populations and their industrializing cities.

Success in farming is always a matter of keen emotion and varying explanation. When it comes to farming the land, no group here matches the Belgians. In the county's hundred-year history of farming, the Belgians are the hands-down winners of getting and keeping the land. Of the 20,000 people that comprise the county, approximately 3,500 to 4,000 people trace themselves to Belgian ancestry; or, to use another measure, 50 percent of the

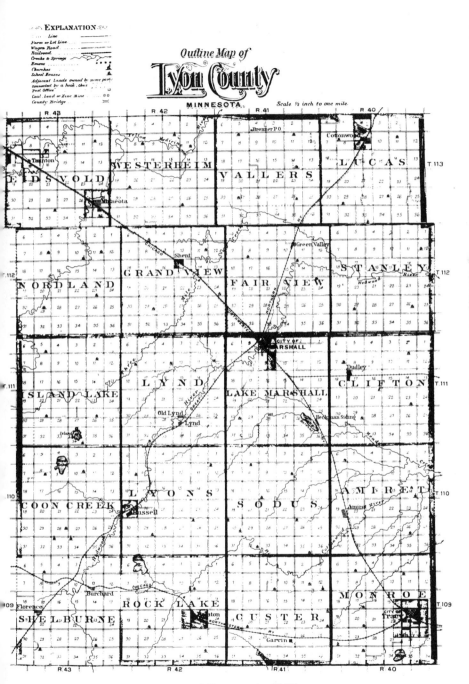

A township map of Lyon County, Minnesota (c. 1915).

county is Catholic and they constitute 40 percent of the Catholics.

The Norwegians, who once clustered along the county's northern tier, simply have not farmed as successfully or stuck to the land as tenaciously as the Belgians. The handful of Irish, Yankee, German and French-Canadian farmers who remain simply don't equal the Belgians in numbers on the land or amount of land held, even though individual families from each of these groups have been notably successful.

The only possible match for the Belgians in the county are the Dutch-Catholics, whom the Belgians call the Hollanders. These Dutch-Catholics, while inferior in numbers to the Belgians, are not easily distinguished from them. They share the same Flemish dialect. Their names are indistinguishable except to themselves or to the rare outsider who has specialized knowledge of the old country. In the old country, they shared borders: 95 percent of the Belgians came from the provinces of East and West Flanders, whereas the Dutch, in nearly equal numbers came from adjacent areas in Holland. This made Lyon County a Flemish settlement; there was a total absence of French-speaking Belgians, the Walloons. The Flemish had a common pre-immigration experience. Many of their family relationships reached back to the old country itself. Since they came to southwestern Minnesota, intermarriage has been common. Both groups came here heeding the call of Catholic Bishop

John Ireland in the early 1880s to establish a mission in Ghent (then called Grandview) and the surrounding townships. Together they formed a Flemish settlement. An 1885 census showed, according to Louis deGryse,[1] that they formed an entirely mixed colony, recording 164 Belgians and 182 Dutch-Catholics in the eight-township area surrounding Ghent and Marshall, the lead city and county seat (with a population of over 12,000 in 1990).

If one were going to propose opponents in getting and keeping the land for the Belgians and their successful Dutch-Catholic cousins, one would have to look outside Lyon county to the Germans who settled in Central Minnesota. Germans extend from St. Cloud in the north, to Glencoe in the east, to New Ulm and even further south and west. One might nominate the Dutch-Protestants, who also came from the proverbially ancient commerce-minded Netherlands. The Dutch-Protestants have admirably succeeded to the south of us. Some teasingly hypothesize that one day they will come to farm the entire state of Iowa.

The Belgians exist in the minds of Lyon County residents on legendary scale. The Belgian farmers are

---

1. Material cited from Louis deGryse, "The Low Countries," *They Chose Minnesota: A Survey of the State's Ethnic Groups,* St Paul: Minnesota Historical Society, 1981, pp. 185–211.

the object of not only jealousy and envy, but admiration, praise, and even awe. In a single conversation, especially when enthusiasms run high, we might hear a rush of statements composed mainly of half-truths and stereotypes. "The only one I know hereabouts who ever paid to have his land surveyed before he bought it, to see how much of it was tillable, was a Belgian." "No one works harder than they do—not even God during the six days of creation." "They never throw anything away—there is no such thing as a Belgian garage sale." "They don't waste their money—the artiest thing about them is their seed corn caps." One question runs, "who is shrewder than a Belgian farmer?" "Another Belgian farmer," is the reply. "They cooperate among themselves like no other group. They even buy pencils wholesale." "Why do all Belgians paint their houses and barns the same color on the same day? They got a good deal on the paint."

Stereotypes of these Belgians, however, are never drawn from common stereotypes of the farmer as stupid, a bumpkin, a pumpkin-jumper, a clod hopper, a shit-kicker, a rube, or what-have-you. If anything, stereotypes of them are drawn from the farmer as shrewd, miserly, cunning, secretive—from the farmer who will bargain on just about anything that might save him money. They are stereotyped as being the farmer who keeps his wallet up in the top pocket of his bib overalls, just below his chin, turns his back to you when he counts his money, and walks and stands in a slouch, for he believes that lightning hits the tallest trees; that is, misfortune usually falls on the luckiest. They still not only calculate, as most do, what is the cost per gallon of gasoline they buy, but even relatively prosperous Belgian wives are heard even today debating the subject of which gasoline brand provides the best mileage. One local merchant suggested that they not only calculate, they'll take all calculations which mistakenly fall to their advantage without saying anything, and even go so far as to play dumb when the subject of the advantageous calculation is brought up.

No doubt, throughout the county and the region there is a low-grade but abiding resentment against them and their success. To my knowledge, however, this resentment never really breaks the surface in the form of direct name-calling or fist-fighting. Statements about Belgians most often reveal a strong ambivalence about Belgians' success in getting and keeping the land. Resentment, jealousy, and anger, along with awe and respect, are simultaneously heard in the voices of those who say, often with wearying repetition, that, for example, you can walk all the way from Cottonwood, a small railroad village of 900 in the north of the county, thirteen miles south to Marshall without ever stepping off the land of the Louwagies, the most prominent Belgian family in the county. A local writer commented, "The Louwagies have been the fore-runners in changing the sky-line of the Cottonwood–Green Valley area with their great silos, three, four, or five to each farm. And so it has come about that when a third or fourth silo appears on a farm, people will ask: Does a Louwagie live here?"[2]

However critically the Belgians are judged, no one stereotypes them as either lazy or dirty. They work enviably hard, in the opinions of most. While one occasionally hears that the funds decisive for their success were supplied by relatives in the old country, this suspicion never implies that they haven't worked for what they have. Indeed, they are most bitterly attacked for overworking themselves and their families. One story even tells how an old Belgian father roped his sons to the plow to keep them at work in the fields.

Belgians pride themselves on their hard work. "You work to live," one Belgian old-timer told me, "while we live to work." They keep their farmsteads up and their machinery in repair. They plow as straight a row and keep as clean a field as anyone; no snow drifts from their ditches (kept equally clean) out into the roads. They are the children of those Belgian and Dutch women who, be it in Brugge, or in old Amsterdam, obsessively wash the stones of the steps and the streets in front of their homes. They are—as I will suggest in the conclusion of this

---

2. From "The Cottonwood Community, 1963," Diamond Jubilee edition, chapter 4, "The Louwagie Saga."

work—a kind of peasant-capitalist, a common breed in the Low Countries.

Positively depicted, they have what they have because they earned it. They keep their word. They are good neighbors. They don't waste their time in town. They are not belly-achers; they meet adversity with resiliency. They go to church. They keep their families together. They are loyal to their spouses, they obey the law, they know how to have a good time (dance and drink), and they can hold the beer of which they are so fond.

There is no end of anecdotal evidence testifying to their hard work and shrewdness. In the downtown coffee klatches of Marshall probably first to mind to prove Belgian industriousness and shrewdness are two Belgian brothers. Each is an accountant-farmer. Each works at one of Marshall's two main accounting firms. Each gets up to do his farm chores before reporting for a day's work, and each returns to farm chores after a day at the office.

The names of business owners also remind Marshallites of the presence of the Belgians and Hollanders. There are the Cattoors, who own three large automobile service stations in addition to selling fuel oil. There is Tholen (a Dutch-Catholic) who owns a large car dealership; there is a Cool who owns a small clothing store and a stationery shop in downtown Marshall, while another Cool sells insurance. There is a Boerboom (another Dutch-Catholic name) who owns a large farm implement dealership; there is a Wyffels (also Dutch-Catholic) who owns a large sporting-goods shop; and there are other Belgians in business, law, and government who figure prominently in Marshall affairs. Also reminding Marshallites how Belgians have amassed capital out on their farms are an increasing number of older Belgian farm couples who have recently chosen to build new and relatively luxurious homes for their retirement in Marshall. A quick glance at names beginning with the letter "V"— a good letter for Belgian family exploration—in the Marshall telephone book yields such common Low Country names as the Van Ackers, Vandams, Van Den Broekes, Vandendriessches, Vandeputtes, Vanderhagens (Dutch), Van de Vieres, Van Hees, Van Keulens, Van Lerberghes, Van Moorlehems, VanOverbekes, Verkinderens, Verschaetses, Vianes, Vierstraetes, and Vlamincks.

There are other signs of the Belgian presence in Marshall. The present state senator for this and adjacent counties is Gary DeCramer. More than any one group, the Belgians dominate Marshall's large Catholic church, Holy Redeemer. (Holy Redeemer was built by loans from Protestant businessmen who wished to signal to Catholic immigrants that they were welcome in Marshall in contrast to smaller towns which were manifestly anti-Catholic.) The prominent place the Marshall Chamber of Commerce has recently given to the annual "world" *rolle bolle* competition during Belgian-American Days, has also called our attention to the presence of the Belgian community. The Belgians brought with them from the old country *rolle bolle,* a game (similar to the Italian *bocce* or the French *boules*) involving two pegs and a beveled disk rather than balls. Representative teams from such distant Belgian settlements as Moline, Illinois, and Winnipeg, Manitoba, journey to Marshall for the tournament.

However, Belgian strength lies not in Marshall but in the surrounding countryside. The land they control in the countryside—and that is what impresses most people—cuts a great swath across Lyon County. Focused in Grandview Township, where Ghent is located, Belgian-owned land extends like a great crescent moon across Lyon into neighboring counties. Belgian land goes from neighboring Lincoln County in the west, across the center and north of Lyon County, to the east into adjacent Redwood County and south as far as the village of Walnut Grove, idealized by the popular television series, *Little House on the Prairie,* based on the Laura Ingalls Wilder stories. The largest concentration of Belgians is in the north central townships of Lyon County, centered in the townships of Grandview, Westerheim, Fairview, Nordland, and Eidsvold, also with significant representation in Vallers, Lucas, and Stanley townships. The only townships showing a minimal Belgian presence are in the southwest, where the terrain is hillier and the soils are inferior.

Joined to a sense of awe elicited by the imposing amount of rich farmland under Belgian control, there is

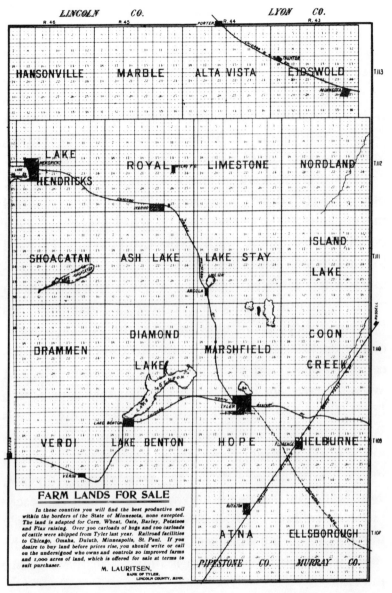

A township map of Lincoln County, Minnesota, entitled "Farm Lands for Sale" (c. 1915). Five Lyon County townships are included on the eastern edge of the map, and Atna (Pipestone County) and Ellsborough (Murray County) townships are shown in the southeast corner.

the additional sense that Belgian expansion is relentless. Only a few Belgian farmers—and they were smaller and newer farmers—got into financial trouble during the recent farm crisis of the early 1980s, when the value of farm land plummeted from approximately $1,800 an acre to below $1,000 an acre, while interest rates soared. The Belgians proved debt-proof; not having to borrow, they escaped the crushing intersection of increased credit costs and shrinking equity. Again the Belgians survived bad times admirably.

The Coming of the Belgians

While ethnic maps have not been completed for Lyon County from its settlement in the 1870s to the present, we have enough information to know that Belgians and Hollanders are getting and keeping the land, while others are losing or choosing to leave it. This process is especially observable from the 1950s onward.

Bishop Ireland purchased the unsold land of the Winona and St. Peter Railway in Grandview, Westerheim, Eidsvold, and Nordland townships as part of his general plan to assure a Catholic presence in southern Minnesota. To it came Germans, Poles, and Irish. The latter failed to take root here, as they did in most other places in Minnesota. At Graceville, another of the communities in Southwestern Minnesota started by Ireland, the Irish, who one year were virtually given land, seed,

13

and horses, were starving by the next spring. Many were former dock-hands and lacked farming skills altogether or were entirely without desire to establish themselves on the land.

To the new settlement in 1882 came some relatively prosperous French-Canadians from Kankakee, Illinois. Within a few months of their leaders having judged the land as being satisfactory, fifty French-Canadian farmers bought 4,000 acres of railroad land from Bishop Ireland's Lyon County holding. They brought with them furniture and livestock, including expensive dairy cattle and work horses rather than the more common oxen. Paradis, Lord, Prairie, Metty, Regnier, Caron, LeBeau, Nevall, Duchene, and Patnoud were names of the early French-Canadian settlers.

In 1881, about fifty recruited Belgian families, totaling about 350 people, started out from the old country for Ireland's Catholic settlement in Minnesota. They sought land for their growing families. Once in the United States, having learned of the dreadful blizzard that hit the Midwest in the winter of 1880, only twelve of the families chose to continue on to Grandview Township in Minnesota. The rest found work in Moline, Chicago, or Rock Island. Among the large families which did choose to come all the way to Grandview Township were the DeCocks, Van Hees, Gits, DeSutters, and Foulons. They averaged six children per family and were most commonly headed by a father, in his forties or fifties, who had some money. They hoped to find in Minnesota the land which they could not attain for themselves and their sons in the old country. These large families, composed of children in their teens and twenties, had the hands to work the land, an important factor if the family was to stay on the land and to acquire more land. If America meant anything to them, it meant the opportunity to own land, which was denied them in the old country.

The Belgians quickly took root. Within a few months of their arrival they had purchased 4,000 acres. In September of 1881, at the immigrants' request, the village of Grandview was renamed to Ghent, an important city of Belgium. In January, 1883, seventeen new families of Belgians and Dutch-Catholics arrived. Among them were the Van Keulen, Boerboom, De Rue, Dieken, Princen, Hennen, Buysse, Maertens, Tholen, and Brewers families. Many were quick to purchase land, build houses, and begin farming.

Father Jules Emile De Vos, who led the second wave of Belgians and Dutch back to Ghent, founded St. Eloi Church. St. Eloi, the patron saint of Flanders, was a sixth-century bishop and artisan, and is commonly known as a saint of smiths and metalworkers.

In the succeeding decades the Belgians came to increasingly dominate Grandview township. In 1885, according to Pansaerts,[3] 98 of Grandview's 430 residents were Belgians; in 1910, Belgians were 356 of Grandview's 680 residents, amounting to a population increase of 263 percent. All groups in Grandview township lost land to the Belgians except the Dutch. Between 1902 and 1914, ethnically unidentified land owners declined 37 percent; French-Canadians 23 percent; Yankees (English-named Americans) 16 percent; and Norwegians 5 percent.[4] In the eight northern townships of Lyon County, Pansaerts computed, Belgian numbers increased in the same period from 154 to 853, or 5.6 percent to 15.9 percent.[5] In Lyon County as a whole for the same period, their numbers went from 163 to 1,086, or 2.05 percent to 6.85 percent.[6]

The heaviest migration came on the eve of the First World War. Lyon County's Belgian population, Pansaerts estimated, reached 1,300 in 1915.[7] The early growth of their acreage in Grandview Township anticipated their success in taking and keeping the land in Lyon County.

---

3. Cited in Carl Pansaerts, "Big Barns and Little Houses: A Study of Flemish-Belgians in Rural Minnesota, Lyon County, 1880s to 1940s," Master's thesis, University of Minnesota History Department, 1987, p. 69.
4. Pansaerts, p. 81.
5. Pansaerts, p. 37.
6. Pansaerts, p. 35.
7. Pansaerts, p. 36.

A portion of a panoramic photograph taken in front of St. Eloi Catholic Church, Ghent, Minnesota, dated June 18, 1933. The occasion was the Golden Jubilee Celebration of St. Eloi's parish.

Already by 1885, Belgians owned 2,040 acres of the 16,633 tillable acres comprising Grandview township. In 1914, they had 9,882 acres of 22,245 acres (or 44.42 percent).[8] They held approximately this amount of land throughout the 1920s and 1930s, a period of great agricultural depression when exodus and foreclosure tried the tenacity of all groups.

The Louwagies

When the people of Lyon County try to explain the growth of the Belgians on the land they frequently focus on one family, the Louwagies. This is especially the case if they seek to understand Belgian growth since the First World War and outside of Grandview Township.

Most people dismiss out of hand all possible rivals to the Louwagies. When I asked one person to compare the Louwagies as farmers with the Buysses, who command a great number of acres in Westerheim Township, I was told the Buysses, as landholding farmers, "can't hold a candle to the Louwagies." Perhaps the Buysses are not considered the Louwagie's equal since the Buysses' ascent to prominence was neither as recent, nor as dramatic, as the Louwagies. Already before the First World

---

8. Pansaerts, p. 79.

War several branches of the Buysses had taken possession of almost three sections of land in Westerheim Township located in the northern tier of Lyon County. Currently the Buysse family holds approximately six sections in Westerheim Township.

Conversations that are driven onward by a discussion of Louwagie success on the land often ignore the favors and benefits the Louwagies received from hard-working and cooperative neighbors. And even more often overlooked is the degree to which the Louwagies—naturally not without some jealousy and resentment—gained, as we will see, control of the fruits of the other Belgian families' hard work and economic cunning through marriage. The Louwagies were never short of children for marriage, and they had more than their fair share of sons to carry on the name.

A certain magic is associated with the Louwagie family. Like any family, that over many generations grows and prospers on the land, the Louwagie family seems special, fortunate, blessed. Their good fortune requires explanation. Why didn't they come undone? What spared them from greed and miserliness on the one hand, or speculation and prodigality on the other? How did they avoid growing jealous and envious of each other, succumbing to anger and hate? How was it that they produced sons who proved to be the equals of their fathers? The unanswerability of these questions adds to the magic associated with the Louwagies. To Stefaan Louagie (Belgian spelling), family genealogist from Brugge in Belgium, this magic extends to the whole history of the family—from the Reformation, when the Louwagies already showed themselves to be consistently good farmers, throughout early modern history when Louwagies were frequently their native village's notary, and even the Napoleonic period, when Louwagies were selected to serve the revolutionary administration.

Hector Louwagie, the founder of the largest of the two branches of the Louwagie family in the United States, was the first-born son of a Belgian family of ten children—eight boys and two girls. All of the children married, with the exception of one of the girls who became a religious sister. Hector came to Minnesota in 1906. He had the support of his uncle Isidore, on whose farm he first worked, and he also worked on the newly established farms of Julius Doom and Ed Coudron in Fairview township.

To the marriages of Isidore and Leonie (Doom) Louwagie in 1901 and Hector and Ida (Callens) Louwagie in 1912, the Louwagies of our region owe their origin. The Louwagies have been prolific and prosperous. They have intermarried with other well-known Belgian and Dutch-Catholic farm families in the area. Success did not spoil them or turn them against one another; instead, they reproduced, cooperated, and prospered.

The Louwagies first settled in Fairview Township, adjacent to and on the eastern border of Grandview

Township. Isidore first purchased 280 acres in 1902. Since then there has been a phenomenal growth of Louwagie land, as indicated by Pansaerts:[9]

Year	Acres	increase (%)
1910	240	—
1920	519	116 %
1931	719	39 %
1940	1235	72 %
1986	4120	234 %

The Louwagies' holdings increased sixteen times in Fairview Township in the period of 1910 to 1986. If the land they attained in adjacent townships is added, their total acreage is increased to 7,780 acres, for a total increase of thirty-one times what they held in 1910.[10] Since 1986, the Louwagies have purchased yet more land.

Rivalry with the French-Canadians

The Louwagies' center was at St. Clotilde's church in Green Valley. They donated the acre of land on which the new church stands, and they have continued to serve and support the church since then. Bishop Ireland named the church after the Queen of the Franks in 1912. But

---

9. Pansaerts, p. 86.
10. Pansaerts, pp. 55–57.

here, as in Grandview Township, the Franks did not prevail: the Belgians again took the land.

The rivalry between the French-Canadians and the Belgians was quite intense in the past. In Ghent this rivalry contributed to a murder. In Green Valley it caused the scandalous incident known as "the blow heard 'round the county."

The rivalry was rooted in the struggle of two cultures. It reenacted the ancient rivalry in Belgium between Flemings and French Walloons, a rivalry which, when over a matter of land, almost invariably witnessed the victory of the former over the latter. But the rivalry went beyond culture. It turned on who would take the land and dominate the community. Heeding Ireland's invitation to come to his Catholic settlement in Grandview, the French-Canadians arrived in considerable numbers, increasing, according to Pansaerts, from 3 percent of the township's population in 1880 to 23 percent in 1895, and then dropping thereafter to 5 percent in 1910. With a few exceptions, the only French-Canadians left in Ghent's immediate vicinity are in the graveyard.

The animosity between the two groups was notorious. It led in the Fall of 1898 to a killing. Already angered by excessive Sunday drinking in Ghent, Bishop Ireland had put the Ghent church temporarily under interdict. A reporter for the Marshall *News Messenger* reported on 23 September of that year: "While it is nothing new for the county seat Marshall to hear about Sunday disturbances in Ghent, . . . a little excitement was created last Sunday afternoon when the constable of Grandview Township, Felix Goyette, a French-Canadian, drove into Marshall in search of the sheriff, to give himself into custody for shooting and killing a man in a disturbance at that noisy 'burg.' " Claiming to square his opinions with what he considered to be "the better element of the community," the reporter contended that the unincorporated status of Ghent and its seven-days-a-week liquor sales made the village "a gathering place for hoboes and toughs from the country around and from nearby villages, and horse races, ball games, booze and drunken brawls and rioting have been the rule, until self-respecting farmers have kept away from the place on Sundays as much as possible."

The previous week, according to the reporter, when Goyette tried to stop two disorderly fellows from carrying on, "one of the fellows gave him a good deal of back talk, and said no — — — French policeman could arrest him." After cautioning them to quiet down, Goyette left for Van Hee's bar only to be stopped along the way by one of the two fellows. A scuffle ensued with Goyette. A crowd gathered, taunting the fighter to "lick the French — — —!" One of the two, Paul Baker, pursued Goyette while trying to grab or hit him. Goyette fired his .32 caliber pistol in the air, warning the crowd to back off. Baker rushed Goyette saying, "shoot me, you — — — shoot me." Goyette accommodated him and shot Baker in the head. Baker's real name was Leopold de Beukaert. He was of "Flemish nationality," and "he who had only been in Ghent a few months, had a bad reputation as a brawling, tough character, having been in a serious row recently in which he threatened a Mr. Princen with a knife and said he would burn his place down." The reporter editorially concluded, "No word of pity is heard at Ghent for the dead man . . . and it is hoped that others will have a wholesome respect for law and order, where before they had none." Whatever the true story here, it is likely that Leopold de Beukaert and the crowd which supported him voiced the animus between Belgians and French-Canadians, an animus which came with some of the Belgians from the old country.

Mainly French-Canadian families established St. Clotilde's parish in 1912, in nearby Green Valley. In 1913 they acquired the original church for St. Clotilde from the Scotch Presbyterians, a group who have since disappeared from Lyon County. Only a few family names remain, reminding us of these once prominent owners of farms in the northeastern corner of the county. In an early church registry, seventeen of the original twenty-nine families were French-Canadian; the remainder were Belgian, Dutch, and Yankee. However, already by 1914, the French priest—who was important to the French-Canadians—had been replaced by a Belgian or Dutch priest, George Vander Velden, and by 1919, marking the dominance of the Belgians, Isidore Louwagie became the church treasurer. During that year, Joe Gregoire, a French-Canadian—perhaps reacting to the appointment of one more Belgian and what he took to be another show of favoritism to the Belgians—one day after mass, in front of the church, hit the priest and knocked him down. This was the blow heard around Lyon County.

"Big Barns and Little Houses"

Carl Pansaerts and I asked Hector Louwagie's oldest, and thus most-trusted son, Marcel, why in the end the Belgians got the land and the French-Canadians lost it. Born in 1914, Marcel was the oldest son in a family of seven boys and three girls. Marcel, like most of his farm contemporaries, did not finish high school, going only through the eighth grade at St. Joseph's Academy in Marshall. There was too much to be done on the farm to stay in school. Marcel married Theresa Boerboom in 1938. Ten years after Theresa's death in 1962, he married in 1972 Ida (Doom) Monnet. Marcel and Theresa imitated father Hector's and grandfather David's families by size and sexual distribution. They had eight children—five boys and three girls. One of the boys died young, another entered the priesthood, while one of the girls became a sister-nurse of the Order of the Sisters of St. Joseph. The rest of the children, showing the tenacity of their tradition to get and keep the land, farm in the immediate vicinity of Green Valley. Marcel's oldest son has thirteen children.

With a slight smile Marcel replied to our questions of why the Belgians got the land and the French-Canadians lost it: "They had big houses and little barns, and we had big barns and little houses." With this common country expression, he told us the classic story (made famous by De La Fontaine) of the ant, who worked all summer and fall, and the cricket, who passed the harvest season singing and dancing. Consequently, when winter came, all that was left for the cricket was the song and dance of summer past. Marcel also explained their own commitment to what has proven to be the oldest rural strategy of all: pour all surplus energy and money into getting more land and the tools to work it.

For Marcel it wasn't primarily a question of numbers of French-Canadians or family size, the number of leaders that filled their ranks, or yet the farming skills or the capital the French-Canadians possessed. Instead, Marcel's explanation suggested that it was of determination and investments of assets. Marcel suggested that the French-Canadians simply didn't dedicate themselves and their families to the land. They liked their singing and dancing too much to succeed in farming on the prairie.

Studies have yet to confirm Marcel's opinion of the French-Canadians. We need to find out whether, compared to the Belgians, they lacked capital and expertise, or the tenacity required for tenure on the prairie; or had

Drawing by Polly Christensen.

they failed to cooperate as successfully as the Belgians had. We also need to ask whether the French-Canadians were too much in love with the smaller settlements of the woods and the more marginal farm lands, all the way north to Quebec and the Gaspé Peninsula, to take to the open expanse of the prairie and its commercial farming.

Quick to Forsake the Land

The same day we asked Marcel Louwagie why the Belgians succeeded and the French-Canadians didn't, we asked life-long Lyon County resident Torgny Anderson to compare the Belgians and the Norwegians—of whom there are so many on the northern edges of the great Midwestern prairie. Of course, we are not implying that all Norwegians gave up on the land. Any plat books from Minnesota amply indicate that some Norwegians do stick to the land, and everyone here knows a story, or two, about an eighty-year-old Norwegian bachelor who owns a thousand or more acres of rich farm land, yet still ties his shoes and pants with twine, walks and hoes his own beans, and goes to the barber shop for his sociability, entertainment, and just perhaps for a free read of the newspaper. This bachelor adamantly refuses to consider making gifts to any of his relatives in advance of his death, for fear such gifts might threaten his future security, or because he has forgotten he will die.

Torgny Anderson, while eighty-five, is not such a bachelor. He is the father of a large family of seven children and the grandfather to eleven grandchildren. He was born in 1904. He belongs to one of the oldest and most prominent Norwegian families in the county. Some of its members once went to Saint Olaf College like Torgny himself, where he had a chance to study with Ole Rölvaag, author of *Giants in the Earth* and a crucial founder of Norwegian-American studies. Torgny, who frequently returns in conversation to how hard his whole family worked, did get two years of college education before returning to the farm. In addition to successfully farming, Torgny served on Cottonwood's school board. He had three terms as county commissioner in the 1960s and 1970s and even in his own late seventies was elected mayor of Cottonwood. Torgny is also an amateur local historian, serving as editor of the 1970 county history. Aside from starting a triple play from the outfield, Torgny's most unusual act was marrying Bertha Kerkvliet, a Dutch-Catholic. He did this at a time when Catholics and Protestants simply didn't mingle (most especially in a Protestant enclave like Cottonwood) except perhaps on an occasional Saturday night at Ghent's dance hall, where Torgny and Bertha met.

Torgny was quick to comment on why Belgians succeeded and his kind, the Norwegians didn't. Torgny told a story. Once he came upon a rat caught in a trap. He threw a board at the rat. The trap came unsprung and, once freed, the rat was too stunned to move, so Torgny clubbed him to death. He argued that his grandfather, typical of many Norwegians, was just like that rat. He worked and waited on his small, 40-acre farm, stunned, not knowing what to do next, until circumstances undid him. His grandfather came to this country poor. He got his 40 acres. He thought the most important thing to do was to mow a little grass for the livestock. He did that— and he and his kind were eventually overrun by the changing scale and economics of farming.

Torgny's own father, Tom, took to the land. But in the course of succeeding, he made Torgny and his brothers and sisters, in Torgny's melodramatic phrase, "victims of pioneering." The father became a tyrant in trying to keep the family on the land. He turned the kids into slaves. The tension to make it on the land was never lessened. The work and the discipline exhausted the children, and gave them little heart for farming. To this day Torgny, who considers himself to be an independent thinker, claims he can't kneel in church, even when he wants to, because of this experience. To worship in church is at some unconscious level of his mind equal to bowing down to the tyranny he rebelled against at home under "Old Tom."

The Belgians didn't fight the war of survival, according to Torgny. They came better equipped, and with more money. When they came the worst of pioneering days were over. The Norwegians always felt alone out on the land. While the Cottonwood area Norwegians did form mutual insurance associations (Norwegian Mutual and North Star Mutual, of which Torgny's uncle was the first secretary) and a gasoline-fuel buying cooperative, (which they, in the spirit of many Midwestern villages, proudly assert is "the world's first"), the Norwegians did not cooperate as close-knit families or clans in the manner of the Belgians.

There were other hypotheses too. The Norwegians, with smaller families and less mutual aid among families, chose to work smaller acreages. The old country had not prepared them well for farming the large and open fields that characterized successful agriculture in the Midwest. It had not prepared them for farming composed around distant markets and dictated by the intersection of profits and interest rates. In contrast to the Belgians, who came more or less understanding the ingredients of modern capitalist agriculture and willing to expand their land holdings for the sake of profits and farming opportunities for their large families, Norwegians worked with a finite and more traditional philosophy of the land. They believed a farm of 40 acres, the original size of many Norwegian farms, was sufficient for their survival.

As Belgians believed they were establishing a destiny for themselves and their families on the land, Norwegians—at least in majority—were restless. They were "Heirs of the Vikings," Torgny suggested. They considered farming merely a temporary condition. Unlike the

Belgians, the Norwegians did not conceive the land to be their destiny. They were quick to exchange their land for other opportunities. Norwegians were willing to do what Belgians couldn't even imagine: they cashed in their land to try other things. They were willing to mortgage their land for their chance to wear a white collar and for their children's education. The Norwegians, who as a group had been in the United States a generation or two longer than the Belgians, not only converted land into opportunity but they prized choosing careers more than keeping the land.

Plowing with Pencils

Torgny and I agreed that the enterprise of keeping the family on the land didn't discipline the Norwegians the way it did the Belgians. Norwegians got distracted from what the Belgians took to be the first matter of their lives, their place on the land. The ministry, art, politics, business—the Norwegians didn't keep their eye focused on the land as sharply as the Belgians. Like the Irish, the Norwegians cared far more about public affairs than their place on the land. They might commit the ultimate farming sin of even missing a harvest, Torgny suggested, for the sake of participating in public affairs. While the Norwegians ran for township and county office, the Belgians stayed at home. Ida Louwagie, Marcel's second wife, remarking on how they always stayed at

Little Civic Activity [handwritten note]

home, said that aside from church, they only left the farm for the required meetings of the local telephone exchange. Only as the Belgians came to dominate townships did they reluctantly take up townships posts. While they have occasionally filled a school board office, accepted a post in the American Legion, or held an office in yet some other civic organization, their focus always remains the farm.

While Belgians conceive it important to get on with their neighbors, even when they are angry with them, in effect, Belgians joined little or nothing. In the 1930s, in the heart of the Depression, Belgians did not lose their land, and consequently they didn't participate in the Holiday Association, which, with its tactics of penny auctions and crowd intimidations, dramatically stopped farm foreclosures and even disarmed the law and overran the town of Marshall in November, 1933. The Belgians simply stayed home, worked harder, pulled their belts in tighter, and calculated more carefully. Only in the early 1960s, when farm prices plummeted, did Belgians in Lyon County join in significant numbers the farm organization of the hour, the National Farmers Organization. The NFO's philosophy was to get farmers to sell to the market on a collective basis and its most radical tactics centered on the use of holding actions. The majority of Belgians who joined the NFO and formed the dominant core of the county NFO chapter were members of younger, smaller and less-established families, whose long-term survival on the land was threatened by the failure of prices in the early 1960s. Those who did join the NFO commonly expressed their point of view with the help of the Catholic church's assertion of the right of the family to have a place on the land. Membership in the NFO transformed many of them into members of the Democratic Party. In Hector Louwagie's family some of the younger sons joined the NFO, though most of the Louwagies didn't join the NFO. In one notable instance in Isidore's family, a Louwagie openly defied the NFO holding action.

The more established and older farmers, whose property grew in value during the 1940s, '50s, '60s and '70s and whose direct dependence on price accordingly diminished, were, in fact, ripe candidates for the Republican Party. Also pushing them in the direction of the Republican Party in the 1970s was the vociferous anti-Communism of Green Valley's Father William Marks, rector of St. Clotilde. The Democratic Party's official adoption of a pro-abortion platform in the same period added increased incentive for Catholic Belgians to become Republicans.

Aside from the earlier election of a single county commissioner and a sheriff in the 1970s, the Belgians only clearly emerged into positions of regional politics in the 1980s. James Boerboom, of Dutch, Belgian, and Irish ancestry, was elected to the State House of Representatives for a two-year term from 1984 to 1986. He, in turn, was defeated by Norm DeBlieck, a Dutch-Catholic in 1986. DeBlieck had previously served from 1982–1986 as county chair of the Democratic Farmer-Labor Party. In the 1980s, Gary DeCramer of Ghent was elected for two four-year terms to the Minnesota Senate where he still serves. More recently, in 1988, three Belgians—Donata DeBruyckere and her rivals, Charles Louwagie and Clarence Buysse—contested for a single county commission seat representing Grandview, Fairview, Westerheim, and other townships.

As other groups adopted the modern formula of equating the good with individual opportunity and happiness, the Belgians' root equation remained the same. They continued to identify the good as getting and keeping a growing family on the land. The family for them has essentially meant father and mother, grandparents and children. It is family in this sense which merits one's most important sacrifices and gifts and contains one's deepest secrets. A Belgian might socialize with a cousin regularly, yet purposely keep his bank account out of a bank where his cousin works to keep the immediate family's money secrets one's own.

This equation also meant not only did they work the land but they calculated it as well. The pencil was as important to them as the plow. "Their houses," said someone who knew the Louwagies intimately, "were filled with sharp pencils." "They couldn't spell, but they sure could add." "They never used calculators; they did their arithmetic in their head, real fast." Their calculations included how to get the land, how to make it profitable, how to best transfer it for the economic growth and satisfaction of the family, and how to pay the least taxes. Through marriage and death they kept their land in units large enough to support a family. While the world around them looked increasingly away from the farm to new forms of work and pleasure, the self-imposed discipline of getting and keeping the family on the land continued to shape their character and lives, as well as determine their farming strategies and their family order.

Their single-mindedness about the land should not be construed to suggest that they are a pleasureless, mean-spirited, or miserly people. An Irish farmer, who has spent decades farming next to the Louwagies, testified to them as fine neighbors. They keep their word and they are always willing to help out. They treated their hired-hands as well as they did their own sons. Another Belgian from a smaller and landless family remarked positively of the Louwagies, "They worked hand and hand with their hired man just as if they were equals. They didn't come to town and leave the work to him." He added, "They are good operators."

The Belgians, while keen calculators, are not a dull and dreary people. They are social. Some even say they are clannish socially, though not economically. They like their beer, cards, rolle bolle, dances, and parties. They always found room for pleasure as long as it was after chores. As noted previously, Ghent had always been notorious for its Sunday celebrations. Years later, in 1933, when given the chance to vote locally to repeal the Prohibition, the vote from Ghent was a resoundingly unanimous 66 to nothing to repeal it. (The Silver Dollar, one of the two remaining bars in Ghent, claims to have taken in the first legal dollar spent on alcohol in Minnesota after the Prohibition.)

Pleasure for the Belgians, however, had its limits— and that was the work which could be done from sun up to sun down. One of Isidore's sons remarked what a waste of time and money going to town during the day was.

For instance, the Belgians continue to keep livestock long after most others in our area have sold off their animals. George DeSutter, who still lives on a long-established farm just south of Ghent, remarked, "He who gives up his animals eventually gives up his farm." The Louwagies stayed with dairy farming even when many of the county's farmers chose the easier life of being a grain farmer, and they stayed with sheep raising when most of their fellow farmers had quit sheep farming. Livestock meant more work and less free time. More importantly, it also meant not having all your economic eggs in one basket. When grain was cheap, you fed it to your animals. Egg and milk checks also had the advantage of providing a regular cash flow.

The Louwagies specialized in cooperative and bulk buying as a family. Hector would go as far as the Twin Cities to arrange for train-car loads of lumber, or other goods to be shipped to Marshall. They were good at bargaining and they have been known for using their collective buying power for everything from food and clothing to farm machinery and cars. One rather fantastic story describes how at one time in the distant past the Louwagies brought a whole trainload of cattle from Montana to share between them. Relatives of the Louwagies are known in the recent past to have sent beef cattle by plane to Japan. Similar to the proverbial Chinese who survived by taking in each other's laundry, to this day the Louwagies sell one another seeds from the same company, which gives them all a commission, and thus, a discount on their own seeds. At the extremes, as contradictory as it seems, this commitment to cooperative buying still means that an individual family shopping for a car will knowingly pay a higher price for the sake of maintaining an established relation with a dealer.

Following their general attitude about consumption, the Belgians guarded against buying machinery and equipment they didn't need. In the early days they shared the machinery they bought. Hector's sons hauled their machinery from one of their farms to another. They purchased adequate, but not necessarily the best and most expensive machinery. One person said that their machinery was "solid but not extravagant."

They have proven to be progressive people by the measure of the adoption of technology. They were far from the last to use horses. They started one of the earliest rural electrification projects in the area. In 1918 about a dozen Ghent farm families (the majority Belgian and Dutch) built their own power lines to bring themselves electricity. Even though the Belgians are modest about showing their wealth, they are proud of a new tractor and combine. An occasional family photograph features the family gathered around a large tractor or combine. They have not hesitated to adopt what machinery they believe to be profitable for their farm operations. And they have also learned to repair their own machinery, an increasingly essential skill for survival on the family farm.

The skills they were most likely to leave the farm to acquire were skills essential to running the farm. They learned to weld, to keep books, to understand tax laws and government programs, which account for a lot of farmers' wealth and tax advantages. In high school, they often studied subjects related to farming. Vocational programs were a preferred course of study for those whose education went beyond high school. Their minds were always turned toward the practical—education was tied to working the land.

At the heart of their success on the land has been an insight which has been shared by shrewd farmers and business people since time immemorial. They knew that money either works for or against you. With this insight came several truths which the Louwagies have exemplarily kept in mind. Belgians didn't spend what they didn't have to. They minimized the farm labor they hired by having large families. Whenever possible, they substituted work for money. They calculated their borrowing. When they needed to borrow money, they first borrowed from each other, which allowed the lowest interest rate, and more importantly, kept the cost of interest in the family. When more land was needed, they usually bought it rather than rented it. They bought the land in small units which they could afford rather than in large units which would seriously indebt them. They bought land outright, or paid in advance as much as they could to avoid paying interest and becoming the banker's slave. The Louwagies took risks only on the land they worked or on the credit notes of immediate family and, in select instances, relatives. For example, at the time of Hector's death in 1959, he had no stocks and only enough insurance to pay for his burial. While minimizing risk, Belgians successfully put their assets to work for them. In another instance, in a period of twenty years Isidore Louwagie took and satisfied 75 mortgages on his home property, which implies that he leveraged his wealth to its maximum for short-term credit.

A friend of mine, trying to summarize their economic intelligence, argued that, in a nutshell, "They were averse to debt. They only bought what they could afford." Their aversion to debt, as my friend surmised, showed in the way they purchased land. They bought acreages in small bites—forties and eighties, rarely quarters—so their credit could digest their expanding purchases. While, significantly, only a few small Belgian farmers went under during the recent farm crisis of the 1980s, what eventually convinced the Belgians that it was a crisis is not that they saw themselves losing their farms, but that they saw themselves, if things kept on going as they were, having to borrow money on a long-term, high-interest basis.

Consistent with their aversion to debt, Belgians minimized their spending for all things other than farming the land. This showed in their preference for "big barns and little houses." They were slow to spend money on their houses and person. A house was for them first and foremost a place to live in. At the start of their marriage they often lived with relatives or in trailers in order to save the money they needed for a down payment on the land. When a Louwagie farm place burned down in 1950, the family lived in the church rectory and the hired man lived in the garage until their home was rebuilt.

Their homes generally are not places of great comfort, nor do they display the wealth that many contemporary farmer's homes do. As one would expect of a people whose labor and capital is invested in their barns rather than their houses, there is an absence of frills in their homes. One senses when entering their homes the world of the 1940s and '50s. Most often their homes are older, two-story wood structures or newer, small, wooden ranch-style homes. Few of their homes have any special rooms added or fancy woodwork. Their builders were not required to provide children with a bedroom of their own, or the parents with an elaborate bedroom, joined by an elaborate bathroom. The parents' bedroom, like other Catholics of older generations, was likely to have a dresser with a mirror, on which stood a candle, a statue of the Virgin with a rosary in her hand, a rosary, and perhaps other religious objects. This served as the household shrine.

Privacy and comfort were not seen as important enough to build modern spacious homes like farmers of equal wealth from other ethnic groups were prone to do. Their homes, like those of traditional farmers throughout the region, are still not likely to have a modernized kitchen, a large family room, a study, or a fancy bathroom.

Although many of their homes may contain a piano, few have furniture which could be described as more than minimal and adequate. They do not usually have glass cabinets, hutches, and other specialized cabinets for displaying a wife's accumulation of fancy knick-knacks, cups and saucers, Hummel figurines, and so on. While possibly covered with wallpaper, the walls of their homes are Spartan. They are commonly decorated with numerous crucifixes (which might have holy palms wrapped around them) and pictures of sacred scenes—and just possibly a shiny neon nature tapestry featuring pheasants or elk. There are few books in their homes, and a minimal number of photographs decorate the living room. The photographs are usually sitting on a small book case, or a round table covered with a table cloth. The photographs are only sufficient in number to identify each member of the family at some important point in his life such as graduation or marriage. In contrast to the modern middle-class home, idealized—even advertised—as the bastion of privacy, individual achievement, comfort, and sufficient wealth, the Belgian home, similar to the agricultural dwelling of times past, is committed to the more modest end of economically serving as the living quarters of the family on the land.

As the Belgian man disciplined himself to the land so too was the family disciplined to the needs of the land. Marriage and death, as we will see, were understood to be inseparable from the family's well-being. For instance, Hector and his children never doubted that a good family was based on a prosperous marriage. His own marriage to Ida Callens produced at least 280 acres of inheritance in the 1920s. Each of Hector's own sons (with the possible exceptions of Charles, who married non-Belgian Carole Christopherson in 1946, and Rene, who married in 1941 a Dutch-Catholic, Bertha Meulebroeck) married into established Catholic families like the Boerbooms, Van Udens, Noyes, and the Bots.

Belgian men never doubted that the farm rose or fell with a good wife. If the father were to be respected, the wife was to be loved. Wives were never in doubt as to what their responsibility was: produce children and support the family on the land in all possible ways. Belgian wives worked hard at tending their homes, children, chickens, gardens, canning, and even taking care of the cows and pigs. They had little free time. When the automobile did arrive, it did not provide an escape to the village, clubs, and hobbies for the women. It simply added yet new chores to the wife's duties—being sent to town on errands and hauling kids—without freeing her of her already large allotment of work. Critical outsiders say that Belgian men have always worked their women too hard. Common gossip in the northern tier of the county charges two young Belgian men with working their wives so hard in the family milking operation that both wives have been damaged for life, one with arthritis and the other a bad back.

Belgian wives serve to this day the family's strategy for getting and keeping the land. The house they commanded was not theirs but the whole family's. Young brides often lived with their in-laws, and as frequently welcomed their mother-in-law or father-in-law into their homes for the rest of their days. The doors of the family home were open over the years to grandparents, the children of relatives, and hired help. On any given day, wives had to be ready to cook for unexpected guests as well as be prepared to serve the local priest who, thanks to the husband's generous invitation, might become a sort of non-paying boarder. To this day women stand as their men, children, family and friends eat.

There are still at work powerful forces to conform to the old way. A young Belgian wife might still feel it her responsibility to please her father-in-law by saving money to buy a few acres of land.

Children were also dominated by questions of the family's well-being. Their childhoods, as would be expected, were measured by and sacrificed to the well-being of the family on the land.

Family energies and savings were not directed to the children's development. Long trips and vacations, special summer programs and camps didn't exist for Belgian youths. Children belonged to the family, not vice-versa. Many Belgian children as recently as the late 1950s and 1960s only had a mattress, not rooms of their own. For the majority, education was understood to be second to farming. Most young farm men didn't finish school. The Louwagies of Marcel's generation quit school between the eighth and tenth grade. School activities were not allowed to stand in the way of farm chores. One middle-aged Belgian woman told me that in her house, there was a simple rule to determine which school activities she and her brothers and sisters could participate in: "If you can't come home on the bus, you can't do it."

A telling instance of change, however, is the story of a friend who, when in high school, longed to play football but his father wouldn't permit it. He asked an older brother who had just that day returned from Vietnam to intercede with his father for him. That evening the older son told the father if he didn't let the youngest son play ball, something which he himself had been denied the chance to do, there would be no son left to take over the farm. The older brother could not have made a stronger argument; the youngest son was allowed to play football but the father never understood the young son's enthusiasm for sport. The father did understand, however, that after getting a college degree in mathematics, the younger son chose to work the land.

The family generates intense loyalty, a loyalty that can be marked by both love and resentment. It stems not only from the single consuming passion to keep the family on the land, but also from the sense of equality that this passion produces among family members. Even though, especially among past generations, the father and the oldest son might control the family as a patriarch, nevertheless, in another sense, the Belgian family functions like an economic republic. Everyone works as hard as they can to keep the family on the land. All are equal in this effort.

The Trinity of Faith, Land, and Family

The only claims on the Belgians that rival those of the land are those of the church. Whatever extra time or money the Belgians have goes to the church. Their commitment to their land and family, a kind of religion in itself, is inseparable from their Catholicism. Churches and schools in Ghent, Green Valley, Marshall, Minneota, and Cottonwood, tell the world at large that here in America they have made something of themselves. Here they built their own churches and schools.

The church, above all else, is a place for them to pray for themselves and their ancestors. It is the place where their sufferings are consoled and where they seek good luck and blessings. Their faith guarantees, justifies, even sustains the efforts of, the family on the land.

Their church is not about new ideals and sensitivities to man and the world. It is about such traditional Catholic concerns as priests and sacraments, grace and perseverance. The priest comes and blesses their homes. In times of drought he leads them in prayer for rain. He holds special Christmas and Easter services to bless their farmsteads.

If they sacrificed their family and money to anything other than getting the land, they sacrificed it to the church. While Louis deGryse is correct to suggest that the Belgians' "loyalty was to the land," he underestimated the numbers of sons and daughters that Belgians offered their church by counting only the priests who came from St. Eloi parish in Ghent. He overlooked the sons and daughters from Holy Redeemer in Marshall, St. Clotilde in Green Valley, Minneota, and Cottonwood who, as priests, sisters, and religious educators, chose to serve the church. The land, the family, and the church is their trinity: one is not easily defined free of the other two.

Their faith offers more than individual salvation. It turns, as does so much ethnic Catholicism, on the continuity of the family across time. The church is where you baptize, confirm, and then marry your young; where you bury your old and say masses for your dead. The church keeps together what even a successful place on the land cannot.

Isidore (named after the patron saint of farmers) and Leonie Louwagie's will reveals the conjunction of faith, economics and family. Written in 1953, the year Isidore died, the will reads as other old Belgian wills do in our region. As if it were the invocation of a prayer, it begins "In the Name of the Father and of the Son and of the Holy Ghost, Amen." The will gave all property to the survivor of the two, with the provision that "the survivor does not remarry." This altogether unenforceable condition underlines how important Isidore and Leonie believed it was to keep the property in the family. Sixty dollars was set aside for prayers for two Gregorian masses for the repose of their souls and another $50 was given to St. Clotilde's priest to say masses for each of them. Upon their death, it calls for an equal distribution of the total wealth of the estate, with land going to the sons and a cash equivalent going to all the daughters, except the one in the religious order. As if to create a kind of Biblical allusion, one-seventh was to be divided into four parts: one part to their daughter Sister Mary Isidore; one part for the Crosier Fathers at Onamia, Minnesota, "to be used by them for the education of priests; and the remaining two-fourths of one part to go to Sister Mary Isidore for her traveling expenses." (When Isidore, who retained Belgian citizenship, died later that year, masses were said, and, showing how carefully the estate had been prepared, Leonie only paid the state a tax of $3.33 on the $18,000 of property they held in common.)

As for Isidore and Leonie, faith, family, and economic calculation were intertwined for all Belgians. The virtues of their faith (love, honesty, patience, loyalty, as well as honoring one's parents) were crucial to keeping the family on the land over generations. Faith strengthened their resolve to endure and grow on the land. It gave them the means to overcome the death of spouses and children, the loss of crops, disease among their animals, the burning of a farm place, and the ravages of summer tornados or winter blizzards. It turned their pains and miseries into worthy sacrifices. It allowed them to transform hard times into a test, out of which they would emerge with yet a stronger will to continue on their way.

The nightly radio rosary broadcast is still sponsored by St. Clotilde in Green Valley. Often it is led by one of Isidore's grandchildren. Until recently, on one Belgian farm in Grandview Township, a small white chapel stood as a shrine of thanksgiving for the end of a disease that was destroying the horses of the region. On many Belgian front lawns one may still observe today a small shrine to the Virgin and a good piece of farm machinery. In more than one Louwagie family, the time is passed during long car trips by praying the rosary aloud, much to the bewilderment and frustration of the children. Praying to have and to be well-off are not dissimilar to them. They are inseparably connected. All this will seem strange only to those who don't understand what peasants have understood from the beginning of time: the land, the family, and the church are as noble a trinity as man can have.

Hector and Ida Louwagie

In the 1930s, Belgians and Dutch-Catholics survived foreclosures more successfully than any other group. In fact, only a very few suffered foreclosures. Already by the end of the 1930s the Louwagie family began to add land. Hector, after working as a hired man, purchased 160 acres in Fairview in 1913, the year of his marriage.

As the oldest son, he most likely received help from his father in the old country. Through his inheritance from his wife, Ida, he added 280 acres to family lands in 1921. These holding were increased in 1927 by an additional 80 acres. In 1937 Hector bought a half section (320 acres) from the Federal Land Bank in Fairview Township; in 1938 Hector and Ida, in two separate transactions, took control of another 500 acres. In 1940 Isidore, Hector's uncle, purchased 40 acres in Fairview township. In 1941, Marcel, Hector's oldest son, and his wife, Theresa, along with Oscar, Hector's second son and his wife, Mary, and Rene, Hector's third son, bought from the Travelers Insurance Company a fractionalized half section in Fairview Township. In 1942 and 1943 Marcel himself purchased another 640 acres from a Mary Bouquet, who in all likelihood was an heir of early French-Canadian settlers. Clearly Hector's branch of the Louwagie family stood ready to take advantage of better times and their ability to work and calculate. As the world entered the greatest war ever, the dream of every immigrant traditionalist farmer was being realized: It was possible to put each of their own children—in Hector's case all nine of them—on the land.

The farmers of Lyon County, and the Louwagies in particular, survived and even began to prosper during the Second World War. With notable exceptions, farmers and their sons took advantage of available farm deferments, leaving the fighting to farm hands, day laborers, sales clerks, students, truck drivers, produce workers, and other children of the laboring classes. Those without land and money served. (Of the Louwagies, again to make them the example, only Maurice and Leon, Hector's fifth and seventh sons, served in the navy during the war.) Probably very few fathers, especially traditional and established farmers, welcomed the idea of losing their sons to the war. The call of the nation at war or the sons' enthusiasm for heroism and adventure paled when measured against the advantage for the family of keeping the sons at home. After all, sons were workers, food prices were going up, farm deferments were available and local draft boards had a lot of discretion—and it could be easily maintained that feeding a nation at war was every bit as patriotic as any other part of the war effort. (There is not yet sufficient evidence either to make the case that all the farm fathers and sons of all ethnic groups equally assumed that the draft was an ineluctable act of God, or, conversely, is there evidence that any ethnic group of farmers followed a conscious and calculated policy of gaining draft deferments by renting, or buying or opening land or the father's early retirement from the land.)

Having survived the Depression's threat to their land and the war's threat to their sons, the Belgians were ready for the post-war world. Again to take the example of the family of Hector Louwagie: in 1946, Oscar added

320 acres in Fairview Township; in 1947, his wife, Mary Van Uden bought a lot in Ghent to add to the family's holdings. Also in 1947 Hector and Ida added another 80 acres in Fairview, while in the same year Maurice, Hector's fifth son, Charles, his sixth son, and Leon, his seventh son, bought a quarter in Fairview. Rene, the third son, added another 240 acres in Fairview Township. In 1949, Emil, Hector's fourth son and his wife Bertha (Noyes) finally took their turn establishing themselves on 240 acres in Fairview Township.

In 1950, the year Hector and Ida returned from a three-month trip to Belgium and Rome, they had every reason to be proud. They had realized America's promise. They had established all their children on the land. Both the boys and the girls had farm places of their own, had married in the faith, and were reproducing themselves and the vision. The girls, Marie, Bertha, and Anna, had married members of three old and successful Catholic farming families, respectively the Coudrons, Van Udens, and Verlys.

It is not accidental that in the Louwagie family history, the two photographs chosen to commemorate Hector and Ida's trip to the old country were: first, at the top of the page, is a picture of them being given a horse and buggy ride in the old country, whereas at the bottom of the page is picture of Ida, dressed in fur, and Hector, posed with a large fedora in hand, standing with their father, David, in front of a new car. The photo caption reads: "Hector and Ida purchased this auto when they visited their home country, Belgium, and left it there for Grandpa David to enjoy." Ida and Hector had accomplished what they set out to do, and as David drove about in his new car in the old country he advertised the story of how well his son, Hector, had succeeded on the land in America. He fulfilled the recently-designed family seal, which is comprised of wheat symbolizing growth, the cross of Christianity, and the horse symbolizing farming.

Before his death (in 1959) by cancer at age 71, Hector added further to the growth of his family in the 1950s. Oscar and his wife added another 40 acres in Lucas Township; in 1952, Hector added another 80 acres in Fairview Township; in the same year, Theresa, Marcel's wife, added 200 acres in Lucas. In 1954, Rene, Oscar, and Emil, again utilizing the tool of collective buying, purchased another 170 acres in Fairview Township. Mary A. Louwagie's name (Oscar's wife) appeared on another quarter in Vallers Township in 1955, and another 200 acres in Grandview Township in 1959. Oscar, perhaps proving himself to be the most speculative of the family, added yet another 40 acres to his land. In 1956, Charles and his wife, Carole, assumed joint tenancy over an additional 80 acres.

Hector's will, drawn up a month before his death, was as clear a measure as there was of how he lived and succeeded on the land. With Ida and Marcel as its executors, the main characteristic of his will was economic equality: his sons should share the land and crop on the condition that the daughters each be given a sum equal of one-tenth (Ida, in addition to the nine children, made a whole) of appraised value of his whole estate, which was inventoried and valued by Marcel and Ida for probate at approximately $150,000. Counting as one half of the appraised $68,000 in joint property he held with Ida, he was worth $107,000 in real estate; $43,000 in personal property, of which $10,000 was in cash and uncashed checks, including approximately $6,000 in notes from personal loans to his own children and nephew Camiel; $8,000 in farm machinery, $6,000 in feeds and grain, and $17,000 in livestock. Having deducted $3,000 for the funeral, $4,000 in legal fees, to be noted, $1,600 in accounting fees, $2,000 in taxes, and $14,000 of claims against the estate, each child and Ida inherited from approximately $9,000 to $11,000 depending in the boys' case the quality of the land they inherited. Showing the care and equality of distribution each child paid a tax of $97.55. In addition to the spirit of precise calculation of equal shares and perfunctory treatment of the church—a $100 donation for "the purpose of having holy masses said for repose of my soul"—consistently in evidence in the will was the amount of self-abnegation which underlay Hector's fortune. At his death, he had one car, a 4-door 1954 Chevrolet, estimated at $450, household furniture valued at $500, and clothing of no market value whatsoever.

The principles which governed the distribution of Hector's estate governed that of Ida's as well, when she died in 1966, at the age of 75. Her total worth, which again so clearly underlines the equality of the sexes in property, was almost identical to Hector's. She had upon death $149,000, of which $136,000 was real estate and $13,000 personal property, with $7,000 of that in her checking account. Her personal goods—which were divided into thirds for her daughters—were without monetary significance; the whole estate divided into stock units, gave one-seventh to the boys, upon the basis that each of the girls be paid $11,000. Again expensive attorney fees, more than $3,000, were required with approximately $2,000 for federal taxes and another $2,000 for funeral expenses. Only the church was the recipient of her charity: $1,000 was given to St. Clotilde, $200 was given for masses for the repose of her soul, and $1,000 each was given to a nephew who was a priest in the old country and a grandson, Vincent Louwagie, who was a priest. As in Hector's estates, the principle of the perfect economic republic on the land was preserved.

Peasant-capitalists

The Belgians in general and the Louwagies in particular remind me of what French historian, Jules Mich-

elet, wrote on behalf of his much-loved French peasants:
"Those people love only the land! That is the sum of
their religion! They worship only the manure on their
fields." "Remember," he explained, "how for centuries
generation after generation have given the land sweat of
the living and the bones of the dead." Michelet had great
sympathy for the father who instructed his son, "You will
live or you will die, my son; but if you live, you will have
the land."

To some extent these Belgians are classic forms of
the European peasant. Like peasants everywhere in the
world they belong to the earth they serve. The world
they know is the land, the family, and the church. Despite
basic revolutions in ideas, sensibilities, and technologies
which have swept the modern world and mind, the basic
horizons of these Belgians were those of the traditional
peasant.

The truth of how much they have remained peasants
is even revealed to them when they returned to the old
country. There they discovered—at least Cyril Viane and
his children did several years ago—that their relatives
living in Belgium are rich, widely-traveled, educated,
able to speak several languages, refined, cosmopolitan.
They don't have bodies and hands made large and thick
by decades of work. Their relatives had exchanged a
hard life on the land for softer and more refined lives in
the city. In the mirror of their old country relatives,
Belgian-Americans can see themselves having gone to

PLEASANT OCCUPATION — B'AKKEN BROS. FARM

A woman feeding chickens, entitled "Pleasant Occupation—B'akken Bros. Farm." A photo from nearby Brown County (c. 1900).

America to remain faithful to the old world their European relatives had long ago abandoned.

These Lyon County Belgians are not that different from my grandparents from Sicily, who under the shadows of Chrysler, worried about jobs and houses, continued to work their gardens and make wine, and prayed to God and used the church to help them and their families. The Belgians acted upon—indeed they embodied—the oldest wisdoms of European agricultural society. They knew you had to work to survive; there was no victory for those discouraged by work or misery. The only dignified way to live and die was to work right up to the end. They understood that all could be lost to taxes and conscriptions of one sort or other. They knew what every peasant knew in his bones since time immemorial: there is no survival except on the land. If you don't have a place in the family which is on the land, you don't have a place anywhere on this earth. Without land, you are nobody; to quote an Italian proverb, "He who hasn't, isn't." The Polish proverb also echoes this sentiment: "A man without land is like a man without legs— he can move around but he never gets anywhere."

Peasants knew that survival depends on the family; all members' desires have to be sacrificed to the family. Individualism, privacy, and intimacy remained secondary considerations for them. They disciplined their interests, energies, and values to the most immediate matters. Their religious faith itself was molded to their need to survive as a family on the land.

By getting and keeping the land through varying economic conditions and circumstances of twentieth century America, these Belgians showed how successful old truths can prove in the new world. They belied the idea, as European peasants have since the Middle Ages, that humanity had to wait for capitalism to be motivated by the spirit of rational calculation.

However, in another sense, southwestern Minnesota's Belgians were not peasants at all. They were imprinted not just by the truths of survival of the old agricultural order, but were also guided by the principles of modern capitalist agriculture and the market. They were conditioned to be flexible, which permitted them to be able to survive in an economic environment in which understanding variable cash flows and interest rates, changing markets, and developing estate laws, was every bit as essential to the survival of the family on the land as hard work, sobriety, and frugality had previously been. Their mind-set was prepared for commercial agriculture. They exploited the land as quickly and fully as they got it. They plowed straight, long lines, with no sentimentality about old farmsteads or concern about the reproduction of wildlife. They worked hard but knew hard work was no substitute for counting. Like their fellow Netherlanders, the Belgians are not easy to sentimentalize as family farmers. They have proven to be exactly what contemporary agriculture demands a successful tiller of the earth to be: farmer-accountants.

Commercial farming was their inheritance and it is their legacy. Right from the beginning of agriculture in the Low Countries, Belgian farmers were in the proximity of major urban centers and ports. They were among the first in Europe, since the twelfth and thirteenth centuries, to know the value of money. They knew the ways of the market that stretched from the ports of the North Sea to the thriving cities of the Italian south. The Belgians who immigrated here at the end of the nineteenth century were not poor outcasts from an ignorant, and destitute land. On the contrary, they were ambitious and they came from not only a rich country, but the richest and most commercially agricultural provinces—East and West Flanders—of that country. There land was expensive and scarce; farming was economic and competitive. Those who came here wanted a change and they were prepared to compete. They worked and counted accordingly, adopting what strategies were necessary over a hundred years to keep themselves on the land.

As we have seen, the first Belgian immigrants to respond to Bishop Ireland's call to Ghent were middle-aged and relatively well-off. They arrived with large families. They chose good lands of adequate size for the market. They quickly set up their farms, with a balanced choice of grain and animals. They established their churches and schools, and set to work. They would make a new Ghent.

While their ambition, knowledge, and intelligence made them join the ranks of the most ambitious agricultural immigrants, they were no different than their successful neighbors in the old country. They were identical to the shrewd and tenacious Catholic and Protestant Hollanders and German immigrants of our region who, understanding the realities of modern commercial farming, knew how to get and keep the family on the land. We could say that they shared the same DNA, or genetic make-up.

This DNA, which is coded for work, family, and church, produces a being capable of great social cohesion, unusual tenacity and cunning, and an unusual devotedness to its ends. This DNA is approximated by all traditional rural peoples who successfully maintain themselves in the modern world, defying the disintegrating forces and the condition of brokenness which characterizes so much of modern society.

So far the Belgians—at least as they can be typified by such families as the Louwagies—have not lost their focus on getting and keeping the land, although we must acknowledge that recently we have heard stories about one Louwagie even losing some land to the universally tempting vice of speculation. We hear about one Louwagie giving up livestock and another experimenting with minimum till and not mowing his ditches for the sake of wildlife. And at least one Louwagie has recently gotten married in a Protestant church. We even hear about another Louwagie family in which only one son of many will even consider farming as a career. Yet these exceptions—and there may be a lot more—tend to prove the rule and to illustrate the tenacity of their tradition.

Throughout this region young Belgians are doing what their fathers would have found even difficult to imagine. Some choose to farm without animals or not even farm at all, which one now hears more frequently. A few consider lengthy winter vacations in the south, allocate more and more time to play sports (even golf), spend money on frivolous things for the sake of pleasure and comfort in their families' lives. They begin to consider their wives' and children's feelings and increasingly honor modern demands for privacy, pleasure, and individual development. Now a few even get divorced.

New wives, especially non-Belgian wives, in increasing numbers turn their back on the traditional discipline which kept them harnessed to the family enterprise. Consistent with the preceding generation, wives have smaller families. Economically they are pushed off the farm to work, as the success of the farm depends more on income and favorable credit than labor, and emotionally and culturally, they are drawn off the farm as the idea of spending one's days on the farm is felt to be painfully boring and unfulfilling. Children attuned to the age insist on ever more pleasures and more opportunities, and their parents, like the parents everywhere, are more willing to organize their lives around the children. The children now participate in a full range of school affairs. Belgian mothers everywhere have become chauffeurs. The children are as likely as others to go on to college and university, and to be less and less likely to hold the all important faith that the only way to survive is to survive on the land. Eventually the revolution will occur: individual opportunities and pleasures will come to matter to them more than the family's survival on the land.

At some point these Belgians' DNA itself will be altered. They will no longer be the same ethnic group they were when they came here over a century ago. They, the most modern and most Catholic of peasants, will disappear. But this isn't going to happen right away— not as long as there is valuable land to own in southwestern Minnesota, and they can form enclaves of meaning around the great trinity of God, family, and farm.

Bibliography

This essay was written with a composite of parish records (St. Eloi, Holy Redeemer, and St. Clotilde), court records, county histories, student papers, family histories (the Louwagies, the Boerbooms, and the Buysses), and interviews with Belgian and Dutch residents of Lyon County, as well as those who live and work with them. Also, important interviews were conducted with Torgny Anderson of Cottonwood, Minnesota, and Marcel Louwagie of Green Valley. Recent conversations with Stefaan Louagie of Brugge, Belgium, who wrote a Louwagie family history, and Charles Louwagie of Marshall, have proven useful, as did critical comments by several other Louwagies and their acquaintances.

Written materials of special use for Lyon County and southwestern Minnesota, which are all available at Southwest State University's History Center, include:

Amato, Joseph. *When Father and Son Conspire: A Minnesota Farm Murder*. Ames, IA: Iowa State University Press, 1988.

———. *Countryside, Mirror of Ourselves*. Marshall, MN: Venti Amati, 1980.

Anderson, Torgny. *Centennial History of Lyon County.* Marshall, MN: Henle Publishing Co., 1970.

"The Cottonwood Community, 1963." Diamond Jubilee edition, "The Louwagie Saga."

DeBruyckere, Donata. "You Can Never Say We Didn't Try": A History of the National Farmers Organization in Lyon County; 1962–1988. A senior paper in history, Southwest State, 1990, to be published in Southwest State University History Series, 1991.

deGryse, Louis. "The Low Countries," *They Chose Minnesota: A Survey of the State's Ethnic Groups.* St. Paul: Minnesota Historical Society, 1981, 185–211.

Pansaerts, Carl. "Big Barns and Little Houses: A Study of Flemish-Belgians in Rural Minnesota, Lyon County, 1880s to 1940s." Master's thesis, University of Minnesota History Department, 1987.

Radzilowski, John. "One Community, One Church, Two Towns: The Poles of Southwestern Minnesota." A senior paper in history, Southwest State University, 1989, to be published in Southwest State University History Series, 1991.

Radzilowski, Thaddeus. "Polish-Americans in Wilno," *The World and I.* July, 1990, 648–60.

Swenson, Steven. "Equality on the Farm? Land Inheritance in Lyon County, Minnesota, 1900–1990." A senior paper in history, Southwest State, 1990.

Useful Works on Minnesota include:

Borchert, John R. *America's Northern Heartland: An Economic and Historical Geography of the Upper Midwest.* Minneapolis: University of Minnesota Press, 1987.

Clark, Clifford F., ed. *Minnesota in a Century of Change: The State and Its People Since 1900*. St. Paul: Minnesota Historical Society Press, 1989.

Fite, Gilbert C. *The Farmer's Frontier 1865–1900*. Albuquerque: University of New Mexico Press, 1966.

Hudson, John C. *Plains Country Towns*. Minneapolis: University of Minnesota Press, 1985.

Madison, James, ed., Heartland. *Comparative Histories of the Midwestern States*. Bloomington: Indiana University Press, 1988.

Valuable works on rural ethnicity and rural life are:

Allen, James Paul and Turner, Eugene James. *We The People: An Atlas of America's Ethnic Diversity*. New York: Macmillan Publishing Company, 1988.

Conzen, Kathleen. *Foundations of a Rural German Catholic Culture: Farm and Family in St. Martin County, Minnesota, 1857–1915*. South Bend, IN: University of Notre Dame Press, 1977.

Gjerde, Jon. *From Peasants to Farmers: The Migration from Balestrand, Norway, to the Upper Middle West*. Cambridge: Cambridge University Press, 1985.

Holmquist, June Denning, ed. *They Chose Minnesota: A Survey of the State's Ethnic Groups*. St. Paul: Minnesota Historical Society Press, 1981.

Luebke, Frederick C., ed. *Ethnicity on the Great Plains*. Lincoln: University of Nebraska Press, 1980.

Ostergren, Robert C. *A Community Transplanted: The Trans-Atlantic Experience of a Swedish Immigrant Settlement in the Upper Middle West, 1835–1915*. Madison: The University of Wisconsin Press, 1988.

Shannon, James. *Catholic Colonization of the Western Frontier.* New Haven: Yale University Press, 1957.

Swierenga, Robert, ed. *The Dutch in America: Immigration, Settlement, and Cultural Change.* New Brunswick: Rutgers University Press, 1985.

Thernstrom, Stephen, editor. *Harvard Encyclopedia of American Ethnic Groups.* Cambridge, MA: The Belknap Press of Harvard University Press, 1980.

Van Hinte, Jacob. *Netherlanders in America: A Study of Emigration and Settlement in the 19th and 20th Centuries in the United States of America,* Vols. 1 and 2. Translated from the Dutch by Adriaan de Wit. Grand Rapids, MI: Baker Book House, 1985.

About the Author

Joseph Amato is professor of history at Southwest State University, Marshall, Minnesota. He earned a B.A. degree from the University of Michigan; an M.A. from the University of Laval, Quebec, Canada; and a Ph.D. from the University of Rochester, New York. He is the author of several books, including *Guilt and Gratitude, A Study of the Origins of Contemporary Conscience*; *Death Book: Terrors, Consolations, Contradictions, & Paradoxes*; and recently *Victims and Values: A History and a Theory of Suffering*.

Professor Amato is one of the founders and definers of Southwest State University's Rural Studies Program. He has not only directed and taught in the program since its inception, but helped win major and minor grants for its development. Also, he has supported the idea of Rural Studies with his writings, which include a variety of articles and reviews as well as *Countryside, Mirror of Ourselves, When Father and Son Conspire: A Minnesota Farm Murder,* and a forthcoming untitled study on the Jerusalem artichoke affair.

Servants of the Land was photoset in 12/16 Baskerville type. Production by Scott and Mira Perrizo at Westview Press, 5500 Central Avenue, Boulder, CO 80301.